Please Stop Pooping your pants

Written By Jen Gonzalez

Illustrated By Andi Green

Sweetie, pretty please,

quit cutting the cheese.
You think it's funny when you toot,
but trust me darling it ain't cute.

You are beginning to smell like

a garbage chute!

We are officially out of the never-ending days...

the oh-so precious newborn phase.

Where the addictive perfume exudes from your head

Overshadowing the blow-outs on my bed.

Odors that chemically bond us so tight,

That I don't even try

to put up a fight

when monitoring the status

of your impressive

feces-storing

apparatus.

So I'm passing the torch, it's no longer mine.
Let's stop pretending that it's fine

To poop your pants

each and every time.

I'll give you money...

How about a hundred... all in twenties?

No?!!

What's it gonna take

To end this headache?

Three days in your birthday suit?

Stickers? Treats?

Pirate loot?

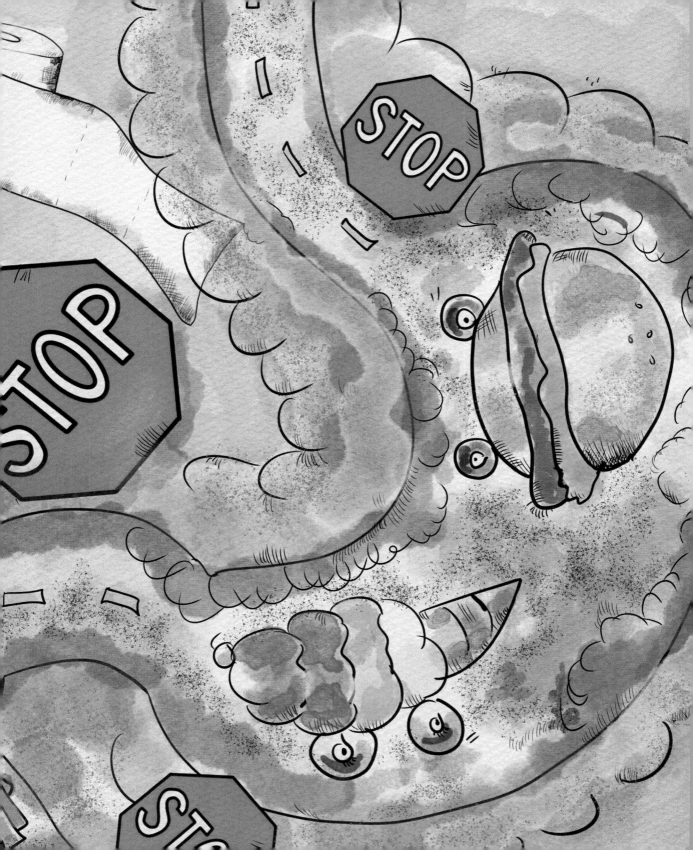

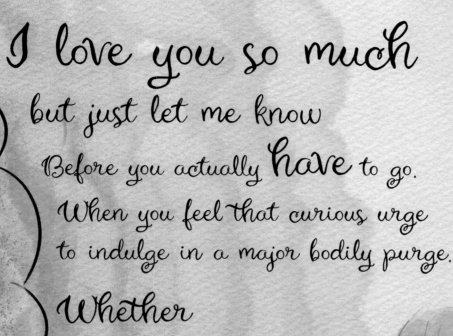

I love you so much
but just let me know
Before you actually have to go.
When you feel that curious urge
to indulge in a major bodily purge.

Whether
on the couch,
in the car
or at the table...

...because Mommy
is feeling
a little

unstable.

And I promise you dear,
this isn't a threat...

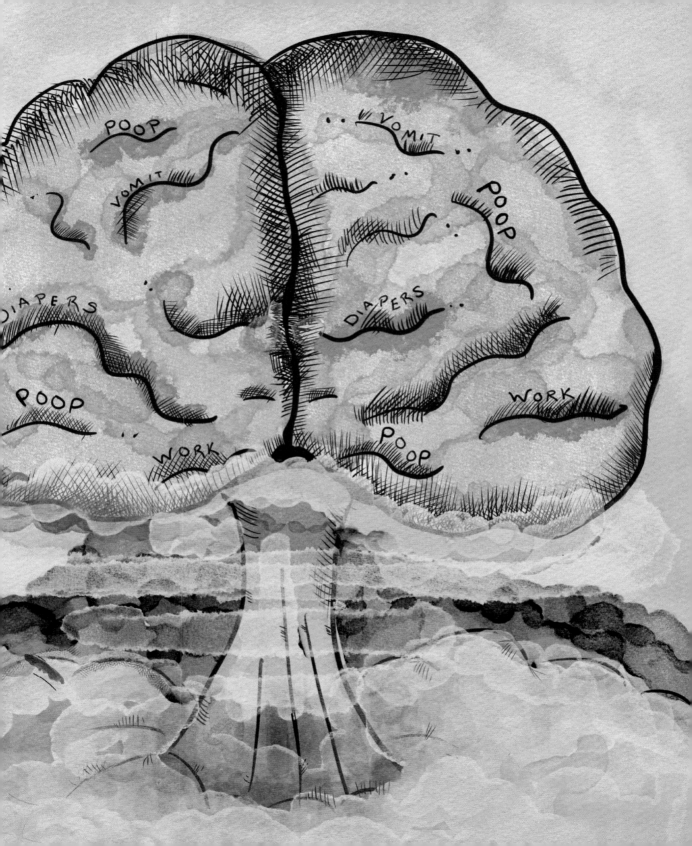

I'm just tired
of placing
this bet.

On how many messes

I'll have to tend

or when this wasteful

diaper phase will end.

I'm trying my best here...
just please use the potty

holding it in
isn't good
for your
body!

I've been as gentle a parent can be,
so you don't grow up with

bathroom
anxiety.

But you have only one job before Pre-K 🎒...

Stop *pooping your pants before you walk in that door!*

I have absolutely zero doubts

That you can quickly end these blow-outs

Who wants to poop in their pants

all the time?

Because we both know

that you'll be just fine...

For one day you'll use all of your smarts,
to listen to your gut making those farts.
And when I see you doing "the dance"...

It'll mean you went in the potty
and not in your pants!

The End

About the Author

Jen Gonzalez is the founder of Doody Free Girl, a colon hydrotherapy practice in Jersey City, New Jersey where she regularly helps clients poop. In an effort to shamelessly open the conversation around bowel struggles and erase the stigma surrounding this very critical bodily function, Jen started the Doody Free Girl blog on her website doodyfreegirl.com in 2012. Jen's goal is to promote both mental and bodily health when pooping!. While it is her life's mission to literally start a Bowel Movement, Jen wasn't prepared for the challenges of potty training a toddler which is the inspiration behind this book. To learn more about Jen and her blog visit doodyfreegirl.com.

About the Illustrator:

Andi Green is an author and illustrator who began her career as a Creative Director in New York City. Andi went on to capture the hearts of parents and educators with The WorryWoos, her beloved series of children's books, plush characters, and educational curricula designed to help kids navigate and talk about BIG feelings. Drawing from her own experiences, Green understands the emotional challenges of potty training, which is why she eagerly teamed up to create a book that openly addresses the ups and downs of helping kids learn to use the potty. To discover more of Andi Green's work, visit WorryWoos.com.

StopPoopingYourPants.com

ISBN
979-8-9870894-5-3

Published by:
Monsters In My Head
PO Box 502, New Providence, NJ 07974
Printed in the USA